AFTER A DECADE POETRY IS PLOUGHED

DIVYANSHI BAJPAI

This book is dedicated to all the folks out there

Whose hearts are tormented......

Contents

Contents

Contents

Poem 1

LIKE A COBBLER HE TRIED
TO SEW THE BROKEN PIECES OF HER HEART
IT DIDN'T HEAL.
IT GOT WORST LIKE A NIGHTMARE

Poem 2

When voices gets unheard
When presence gets unseen.
Like a desperate bard.
She bleeds her unspoken thoughts
And anguish on the vintage pages
With the ink full of desire

Poem 3

Tress shattered their leaves as if.
They wanted to leave that place
Beside the moon I found my happiness
Sitting there with the cup of tea gossiping whole night about
you.
because you are the reason for my happiness.

Poem 4

What if I say grass grows apart.
Does the heart do the same
When its tormented.
Love can never felt like a betrayal or burden.
It's the sour wordings which is pierced like a knife deep inside
the heart.......
Isn't it hurtful ?
Oh!! JANE MAY NOT BE...
BECAUSE EVERYONE DON'T FEEL THE SAME
Like YOUR HEART DOES??

Poem 5

What makes life beautiful ???????
Oh yes sitting with the stars
Talking endlessly without any inferiority;
Than breathing out every scars out in the universe
Which made you suffer like a dead corpse.
To admire every belonging of nature which healed
Your broken part.
To endlessly submerged like a ship inside the deep waters
Which made you realise what makes life beautiful.
There you will find a reason.

Poem 6

One tormented heart is like
Bites of thousand scorpions.
Scars don't heal easily
They makes every breath suffocated

Poem 7

PERSPECTIVE OF MY EYES.
I TILL HAVE TRACES OF YOUR WINGS SAVED IN
MY DIARY
I SAY YOU FLYING.
BUT SOMETHING WHICH DESTINY HAVE
DECIDED FOR YOU THAT
I WAS NOT AWARE OF.
I SAW YOUR BEAUTIFUL WINGS FLUTTERING.
I SAW YOU SITTING ON THE FLOWER SUCKING
THE NECTAR
BUT THAT MOMENT YOUR BREATH STOPPED IN
FRONT OF ME
I REALISED NOTHING LAST FOREVER.
BEAUTIFUL ANTENNAE ROBBED MY EYES.
HOW SHINY THOSE EYES WERE WHICH MADE ME
FALL FOR YOU
THE GLIMPSE OF YOUR APPEARANCE MADE ME
REALISE
BEAUTY FOR SAYING BUT ITS ALL ABOUT
PERSPECTIVE

Poem 8

*WHATS MORE SUFFOCATING THAN BEING A
HUMAN BEING?
I WONDER HOW MANY BROKEN hearts SURVIVED.
THOSE STARS MOCKING AT THEIR DEVASTATED
CONDITION.
TO THOSE WHO HAVE FORGOTTEN THEIR AIM
TO BECOME WRITERS.
THEY ARE LIVING THEIR LIFE AS A DEAD CORPSE.
A BIT THOUGHT STRIKE IN MY MIND WHAT
MADE THEM SUFFER SO DEADLY.
THEY FORGOTTEN THEIR RHYTHMS OF MUSIC
WHICH ONCE OBSESSED BY LOST PERPETUAL
SINGERS.
THEIR HEARTS COULD NOT HOLD THE GRIEF.
IT OVERDFLOWED.
WHATS MORE SUFFOCATING THAN BEING A
HUMAN BEING.?*

Poem 9

Broken hearts wandered thousand miles
Peace they got sitting beside the
Silent trees alone in the midst of the night

Poem 10

if reciting the same story which left
Nothing just an unexpected
Thought of despair.
Consequential to attachments

Poem 11

Before my presence gets mixed in the soil.
Tell the world.............
She loved you as if she never had any other desire.
Than you.
She loved your voice as if she never heard any other voice.
She loved everything about you even your scars.
Your eyes felt like drowning myself inside the deep waters.
Everything felt so serene beside you.
And you are loved profoundly, dearly,
You mattered......

Poem 12

Like eccentric bibliophile
She hunted for one word
And ploughed a poetry after a decade
Isn't it beautiful to deeply
Admire the mysteries and
Unheard folks.
Like searching oysters from oceans

Poem 13

Those tears was not enough to
Show affection towards you.
Those dried roses kept in a resin
Preserved was not enough to show how much
Your memories haunt me.
Wearing that black colour dress
Which I hated like anything was not enough
To make your desire come true
Trees shed their leaves in the
Autumn but I kept your memories in my heart
To cherish them forever.

Poem 14

Hope haunted their body after unwanted grief.
When I look at the sufferings of living heart beats.
It reminds me of the time once like nomads I wandered
thousand miles
Peace my inner soul got sitting beside the hushed trees
Alone in the midst of the night
Is there left any corner for hope?
But for them it feels like desperate urge to renounce ever
sufferings after a while.
But some where their hearts holding a lot of trauma despair
and chaotic grief.
As it is said eyes hold the tears of lament
And the tormented folks feels like buried corpse
What brings peace ?
Place full positive aura, aromatic smell for which folks tends
to release their agony and forgot the pain veiled inside for so
long.
They felt high on the clouds after smelling the addicted
fragrance of flowers

Their pains vanished like water spilled on the soil and the fine
particles get settled down Their souls started

Not only I but that whole world believed in you
Because you try to emit some magical chants
Around.
Some got hypnotize by your presence.
Some became unconscious by your essence
What supernatural powers flowers owns understood
By tormented souls
Their hearts bloomed after observing such a heavenly serene.
Grief lasted their body and hope filled with
Lots of upcoming desires and the casket full of happiness.

Poem 15

TOTALL RECALL OF MY PAST I wondered.
Why I revolved myself around that single gem like the
circulating waves inside the oceans.
It triggered my potential that how coward I still feel
When memories of agony and broken trust revolve around my
fragile heart.
Trust being deprived.
Moreover it caused bursting fire in my head
Which all ruined my soft thinking brain
And the anger in my veins which burnt almost 500 calories.
It freezed my nerves inside my immortal soul
Cuz total recall seemed to be much devastating to me
The pretence of the gem is coated with that fake loved
It seemed.
My two parallel eyes believed in that fake coated gem.
To my perspective world seemed to be the pearl dig out from
the ocean
But in reality it is rusted with treacherous folks.

Poem 16

Footprints?

Admiration needs patience
And ability to discover new unseen treasure
Of the world
World is vast to discover but heart isn't
To leave footprints on every place you go is the best
Way to get through the memories of your past
You left once on the way to your journey

Poem 17

Escapism felt like comforting tides
after chaotic depression from the world.
Where everything feels like knife pierced strongly in her
Heart.
After a while when eruption of lava cooled down
She breathes slowly and said
Let me fly high to get the heavenly pieces of art.
Let me expelled the truths and hatred out to heal it better
What made her pains so disastrous.
What and where from her heart trying to escape.
Like a venus goddess she spoke some heart felt words out.
Like as if she suffered a situation of catastrophe from the
world.
Her wings exaggerated as if she wanted to fly high without
Any obstacles.
But after a decade it feels like a bird that is caged for a long
time
Her thoughts and her desires been snatched.
She unable to fight, her feets tied with some responsibilities
For which she could not escape.
After a while when sufferings could not be hold anymore
She tried to break the chain of tolerance

and social stratification to free herself from being dominated.
World we live in
she suffered like a slave

Poem 18

Forever the body decayed.
Not the deeds.
Corpse buried but not her sweet gesture.
Person buried not her values.
She is not mortal but how her heart made others feel.
Still resides inside those beloved breath taking fellows.
She died not her legacy

Poem 19

If eyes could capture the deadly
Faces of monster
Hiding inside the caves?

Myths symbolism…

Poem 20

My conscious confused with this mysterious world where every
sin.
of living is locked by unsearched destiny.
revolving around the committed sins.
are they really ruled by demonsters.
are they lost where dark angels hypnotized their minds.
what caused world to be desolate like serpents in the jungle
and their mind so sinful.
eyes flowed the volcano and tears lamenting over the sin
committed by the world.
body got hallucinated by the sufferings and the living could
not control their inner dark urge and renounced their
heavenly deeds
to enter the monostrous fantasy.
deprived of the fact lost hearts searching serenity but unwanted
sins crawling over the good deeds.
their mind reciting the deepest lines of buried poem
that is in this Nasty world there stood a slanting tree of
serenity
beside the cruelness of snakes crawling every corner of the dusty
streets
once I looked upon the cloud its saying you lost that charm

when you enjoyed the opera of sophistication.
it is devastated by the hustle brain of demonsters
no calmness, stillness I found.
mystery she unable to plough and the sins buried along
with their corpse inside the grave 20 yard beyond my
will.......

Poem 21

There I see you.
Hope you are fine.
Still longed for you there we stood apart
Once.
Streets are empty and me waiting on those
Lonely streets.
There is something I am unable to forget.
There still something in my crooked heart.
There is you and me.

Poem 22

Life is not about how many
Bruises people have given to you.
Its about who have purely weaved your scars.
And cared about those.
instead of mocking at your deteriorated condition

Poem 23

If every tear of mine shed
Was like a pearl for you
Than why those sea waves lamenting over?
Because everything seemed or said is just
Pretentious.
No real emotion is found ?
Somewhere sea waves heard your conversation
When my presence could not.

Poem 24

if my heart wasn't messy and fragile
Then how would my inner
Soul know the pain
Which kept on rolling.
And got better with shinning sun above.
Our forehead.

Poem 25

In the midst of the night
All I am standing alone
Stardust just rushes with the gush
Of air.
All I need to provoke myself
From day dreaming.

Poem 26

What makes breath intoxicated??
Shingles of reality where people somewhere
Lost their way and the dreams they had in their forever
beloved eyes.
They forget their aims to conquer the world.
Whats more depressing than seeing a person walking
alone on the road full of thorns........
And turned their paths into treachery.
They are being deprived of freedom.
As if demons possessed their minds.

Poem 27

I asked my inner self what makes me happy ?
She says everything cannot be taken as a perspective of
Happiness.
But!!
When trees fluttering their leaves and making
My inner soul realise that after so many scars.
Storm have given to their roots but still they
Stand up straight.
After so many bruises, they still swirling their branches.
She asked herself what makes life meaningful
When sea waves returning to their shore
Enjoying to the utmost.
When little things enjoyed from heart
Without any inferiority called life.
Not by how many fancy you owns.
Just like sitting in the garden and
Observing how flock of thousand birds
Making every moments memorable.
After a splash of memory.
I realised let all enjoy
Every moment without cursing.
Cuz soil waiting to burry.

Every belonging who have germinated through
Its origin.
Free heart from distraction
To live a single breath in harmony.

Poem 28

Love have different forms to address???
It was Wednesday 24 february 2024.
My eyes rolled and I saw a cute little kitten
Trying to hide himself from danger.
Well who can be more dangerous than a human being
The terror in his eyes felt like as if he lost all the hope
To be saved.
But.
Soft paws crawling all over my heart
On my neck his sharp claws making those painful scratches
To prove how much that little baby loves me and my deceptive
aura.
To connect his heart with mine.
Though he knows how selfish , lethal human beings are
Still hope someone will love me out of the way.
Trust being worthy..................

Poem 29

Heaven serene I wondered for ages
It acts like dwelling place for my broken heart.
Where I insist myself to forgot about my
Unreasonable worries.
Which is totally residing inside my brain
It gives me the reason to
Heal my past
I was drowning since
Ages.
Destined my silly mind
Where to focus
Cuz heaven serene seems to
Be much relaxing.

Poem 30

I am hiding myself behind the moon
Its seeking my presence from the
Side of the trees.
It shook its head and
Asked why you looked
So gloomy ?????

Poem 31

Gushing sound as if something
Fallen to my soft brain
But it was nothing more than
My overthinking which leads to the lots of destruction
But wondered?
Why its put to more consideration.
Its heavy like a bulky stone.
Put towards my whole head.
Its dreadful.

Poem 32

Art exhibits in the form of lament.
Where her pens scribble her horror, terror.
On white pages.............
To release unwanted grief from her heart
Which made her like a dead poet

Poem 33

Beauty for saying
But its all about perspective
One says she is beautiful
But could ever thought
What is true meaning of beauty
I wandered miles to figure it out,
Answer I got.
Beauty can be defined in that marshy water
where lotus blooms
Isn't it ??????

Poem 34

Garland woven
from the knitting thread
To behold the love of unseen folks.

Poem 35

How does it feels when dreams are.
Shattered ?
Trust breaks from the contagious world
When they break your trust into pieces.
Like a glass falls from high cliff.
Trust being worthy for her,
Where she defined herself she believed in you.
But if it breaks her heart wont be stitched twice.
When you believed in fake world and
In return what you get ??
Hatred, criticism......

Poem 36

I was waiting for night to come.
Stars are shining.
The loneliness still strike my mind
You were such a bliss at night
Can I stay more longer with you??
How long you seek for unfaithful love
Which only brings agony not the peace

Poem 37

• 41 •

Miserable is not the destiny.
It is you ....

Poem 38

Cry of pitty.
They wore a mask of flowers
But their heart was filled with sticky thorns.

People are deceptive..

Poem 39

His heart or his partially
The same.
Its just the feelings from
One soul parted after a pause.
Deep stories are not grief given
Only.
The endings make the soul eyes burdened.

Poem 40

roses remind me of
the broken pieces of her heart she left there

past memories overflowed from no where ......
oh I remember every depth of faded memories.
I could calm myself but broken pieces of my heart.
Still resides in the garden full of roses and smell of
Your breath reminds me of unforgettable love
And the moments we cherished.
My pains bruises vanishes like vapours when those
Memories haunt me from no where.
They have been stars to my scars,
Aha !!how much I try to avoid but after all they are flowers to
my thorns.
Incomplete memories feels like grief never ridden off
But what makes my heart little laugh is cherished
Moments.
Biggest nightmare I had in my forever beloved eyes to fall
apart
After chasing all the melody of life together.
Was words of wisdom seemed to be pretence or dramatic
illusion isn't it

I remember not those who totally.
Got hallucinated by the chants of cruel voices
But the fact they cannot pour
Their heart full of emotions to the another
Soul?
Aw sometimes I still suspect my conscious to be truly devoted
For the entities who are never meant to be mine.
Oh cara mia!!roses are scattered on the ground with full OF
gloomy emotions.
Does my heart is scattered same LIKE ROSES
Some memories forever in hearts.
Just their prints make souls full of grief
Isn't it ????

Poem 41

She tried to escape like a bird from the chaotic cage
Where everything felt like wild as a ghost.
She stood apart when eyes captured the betrayal
And the hatred from the monster she loved once.
She believed like a saviour and worshipped their
Disgust.
Without knowing their beguile minds.
Their callous act hypnotized her mind
and tried to RULE her presence
Why she being so blind ?????

Poem 42

What if roses could speak?
Their charm could enter the hearts of broken
Souls.
Could have heal the people.
Suffering from breakdown, anxiety
Depression and what more.
Roses are human beings not just the flowers
Roses have some kind of magical powers
To heal the broken bruises…
Some entities makes life.
Beautiful.

Poem 43

• 48 •

When storms could not be hold
Eyes searching for serenity.
While soul admiring beauty
To fully drown he self inside the
Admiration of roses !!
Whats more beautiful than seeing a blooming
Flower…

Poem 44

Eyes weren't lying.
Every precious soul tends to attract from
The well fortified heart.
To those who made another souls realise their worth.
Not those who wants your fate.
Eyes were not lying about the rhythms of love
Which one tends to have with those pure souls.
Numerous souls in the world.
But I will always choose yours jane..

Poem 45

Serpents in the jungle
Got hypnotize by the presence of
Heavenly divas.
Could not emit the poison
For which they are being send for
WAS SHE REALLY SO DECEPTIVE ??

Poem 46

Hii peeps my name is elizabeth.
Aha somewhere you all have read or searched my name
In both books, novels
Do you all wanted to listen my biography
So here it is.
I am from far away where no one could ever go
Some lines wanted to recall about my
Messy journey.
Far across the distance
Where no stars can ever shine.
I am lonely like those shiny stars in the galaxy
Above our forehead.
Walked few miles and turned and diverted from the slide
Road.
My mind crooked.
I can turn up to right and left to up
I can slide my head like a ghost in a haunted jungle
That no man could ever do
I wanted tell you one secret I am unique in a way
But sometimes I do feel bad.
I do have feelings.
I also have to hide my pains behind the moon.

I am broken at times
But I don't have anyone to share
I roam here and there in search of food but at last what she
gets shitty humiliation from nasty humans.
I don't want there luxury house.
I just want a little love, cuddles and little food to fill my
Empty stomach which empty since ages.
Will I get this ever?
Or I have to wander like this in that strong summers in
search of love.
Do I have to bargain for it ?
Will someone will pick me in their cosy hands and say
Sweetie don't worry I am here to take care of you.
God created me but I also need affection, attention
They don't value my presence.
I am not just the cat I am that love which man needs today
My name is elizabeth
I am that shine which will make your dull gloomy rooms
The everlasting memories you could ever think of.

Poem 47

One breath felt like bites of thousand scorpions.

Aha its not the world who made her feel so disastrous.

Its just the heart to be survived here.

What make it broken darling ?

Love ?

Oh no its trust which people break same like the glass

Fallen from a cliff.

How could you be so blinded as if

You never Saw the dark side of snakes mia.

Some folks don't deserve your purity they deserve your betrayal

Pure souls are the most hurted version of thorns existed.

World is false inner self realised.

Trust is just a simple word expelled out.

Illiterate folks don't even know.

Whats true meaning of love ??

It takes thousands year to gain and one second to break it like

cutting down the string apart.

Poem 48

They have eyes but cannot see beauty
They have ears but cannot listen prevailing
Truths of life.
They had beautiful senses created but unable to
Notice the wonders and unseen treasure of the
World.
The beauty of world are only noticed by those insane
Folks who are excluded by the society.

Poem 49

In solitude she started finding peace
When world she live could not
She cried out in anger why sufferings always
Comes to her and never try to leave it.
There across the waters once observed
Sea waves crashing over the stones and
That made the heart full of solace
Its not about how many people crowded its about
Whose presence made you feel over whelmed.
In solitude she found her way.

Poem 50

life is mingled like cobweb.
We do face obstacles same as the trunk twisted because of the
Bruises.
But at the end they teach something tremendous.
Something adventurous.
Do not act like a coward after facing petty obstacles.
Instead try to haunt them as much they haunting you.
Life does not stop for anyone.
Life is crucial at points we do fear out.
Does fearing is the ultimate option for your sufferings ? no.
Sometimes memories of insomnia reminds me of the time
Once we all have stopped once in our journey.
But still there is hope for standing once again like a tree
And try to face where you stopped with patience.
Patience is the ultimate component for every puzzle.
Obstacles act like oregano in life.
They will make you stronger same as the heat of the iron.
They will bring storm inside you for facing most dangerous
Stunts from which you are hiding
You will fight back same like spider fights for her web.
You re not that weak that you will lose yourself without trying
out.

Remember it to fight

Not to stop.

Life is beautiful like a flower that blooms everyday.

And writes a new chapter for you ………

Poem 51

Get your presence so high
Like mountains
So that inner monster could not try.
To Dictate your mind

Poem 52

what hurts the most ?
when our own blood
turned out to be snakes
expelling venom after few months
pretending they loved us.
was everything was just a pretence.
trust be like water spilling on the ground and
vanishing every feeling, concern from the elements

Poem 53

AGAINST THIS WORLD THERE IS NEW
GROUNDED FAIRYTALE GARDEN
WHERE WE MEET IN OUR DELUSIONARY DREAMS.
VISIT THAT GARDEN JANE!!
ALL THOSE ROSES ARE DRYING UP THERE
YOU GAVE ME IN THE MIDST OF THE MOON…

Poem 54

Her heart says
She wants jane forever
But life wants him to get apart.
Her thoughts mingled with the fact of eternity.
She speaks words filled with lament……..
I swear you cant get rid of me
Until I and my soul gets buried inside the coffin.
Was she too attached to him or his presence…….?

Poem 55

Going through the phrase where my mind
Recalls all my worst memory lane,
but those white blossoms it takes my mind to
Somewhere I see mountains.

Greenery and everything I dreamed of.
Pretty eyes thought of once to see the white unicorns,
butterflies in the sunflower garden,
Is it reality or flared dreams?
Nature heals the broken part.

Poem 56

Remember that when

I lose my four senses somewhere.

You will awake me from the horror syndrome

I was facing due to deleterious world.

Time to be remembered

Yes I do.

It was 3.o clock am

Like psychopath

she woke up in the midst in a fumble way

searching for you.

That's why your presence is treasured for HER.

Poem 57

On canvas of life.
She painted her destiny.
Splashed rainbow full of
Upcoming ADVENTURES..
LIKE A PSCHYOPATH PAINTER
SHE TURNED HER FATE INTO
NEW BEGINNINGS..

Poem 58

Inside the graves corpse shouting.
In Agony for lost love...
Weathered skin screaming out for heavenly departure
after physical exhaustion.
For those who died lamenting over misery in love.
How many souls left or criminated without feeling
the presence of love.
Love is beautiful but sometimes.
Is it a curse.

Poem 59

Everyday is a new chapter that blooms
Beautifully like a radiant lily

Poem 60

oh really my love is this desolate ??
I hear the roaring sound of thunder as if heavenly echoes
Wanted to reveal deadly hidden truths.
I guess sea waves in despair lamenting over the fact
That why trust being deprived.
Those desperate roses near the willow trees drying up
Because you broke the promise you did once.
Her heart cant get over that one pretence could destroy
millions of heart.
Wish if her eyes could capture the deadly monsters hiding
inside the caves.
Oh honey, don't shed tears because some promises are meant
To be broken in order to break the chain of trust..........

Acknowledgement

You forget how much time has passed until you sit down to write acknowledgement

When voices are supressed by the society it does not affect you it's the heart that is tormented.

Firstly I wanted to acknowledge my biggest motivator miss caroline who made me realise my worth.

How badly I used to shout on her instead she calmed me told me what I can do.

Every success of mine goes to my one and only mentor miss caroline not just the teacher mother in disguise.

She is the main reason I started my writing journey.

She is treasured to me.

Last not the least thank you all to my fans who asked me to publish my first ever anthology.

Without your support it wouldn't be possible.